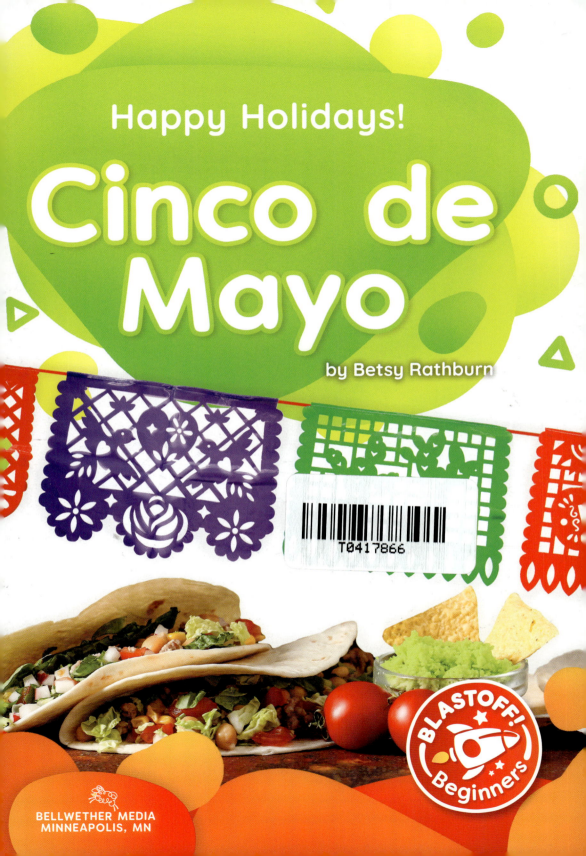

Happy Holidays!
Cinco de Mayo

by Betsy Rathburn

BELLWETHER MEDIA
MINNEAPOLIS, MN

Blastoff! Beginners are developed by literacy experts and educators to meet the needs of early readers. These engaging informational texts support young children as they begin reading about their world. Through simple language and high frequency words paired with crisp, colorful photos, Blastoff! Beginners launch young readers into the universe of independent reading.

Sight Words in This Book

a	go	may	some	up
about	here	on	the	was
are	in	other	there	what
day	is	out	they	
eat	it	people	to	
from	long	play	too	

This edition first published in 2024 by Bellwether Media, Inc.

No part of this publication may be reproduced in whole or in part without written permission of the publisher. For information regarding permission, write to Bellwether Media, Inc., Attention: Permissions Department, 6012 Blue Circle Drive, Minnetonka, MN 55343.

Library of Congress Cataloging-in-Publication Data

LC record for Cinco de Mayo available at: https://lccn.loc.gov/2023001659

Text copyright © 2024 by Bellwether Media, Inc. BLASTOFF! BEGINNERS and associated logos are trademarks and/or registered trademarks of Bellwether Media, Inc.

Editor: Christina Leaf   Designer: Laura Sowers

Printed in the United States of America, North Mankato, MN.

Table of Contents

It Is Cinco de Mayo!	4
A Day to Remember	6
A Colorful Day	14
Cinco de Mayo Facts	22
Glossary	23
To Learn More	24
Index	24

It Is Cinco de Mayo!

Music plays.
People dance.
Cinco de Mayo is here!

A Day to Remember

Cinco de Mayo is on May 5.

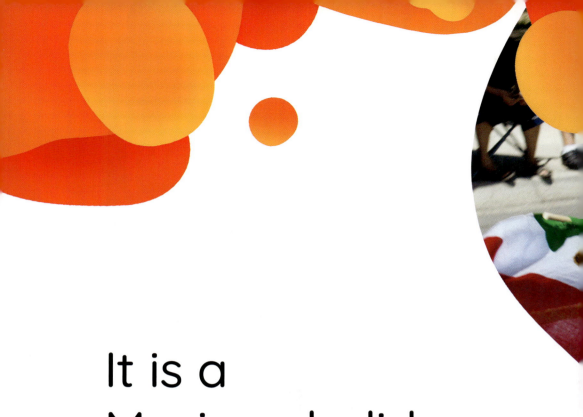

It is a
Mexican holiday.
Others join, too.

It honors a **battle** from long ago.
It was in Puebla.

Puebla, Mexico

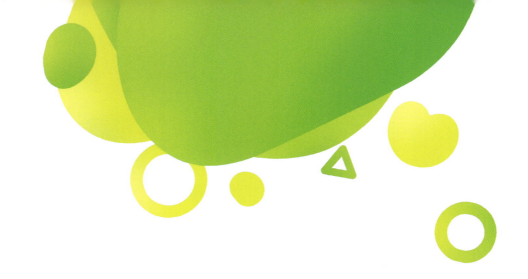

The day also honors Mexico.
It honors life there!

A Colorful Day

People learn about the day. Some act out the battle.

People hang colored paper. They put up paper flowers.

colored paper

People eat Mexican food. Tacos are tasty. **Mole** is, too!

tacos

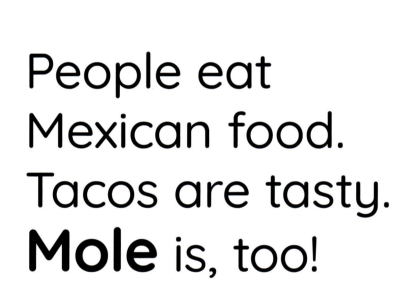

mole

People go to **parades**. They dance to **folk music**. What fun!

folk music

parade

Cinco de Mayo Facts

Celebrating Cinco de Mayo

colored paper

tacos

Cinco de Mayo Activities

act out the battle

eat Mexican food

go to parades

Glossary

battle

a fight between armed forces

folk music

music passed down from long ago

mole

a sauce used in some Mexican foods

parades

people or groups who walk together during events

To Learn More

ON THE WEB

FACTSURFER

Factsurfer.com gives you a safe, fun way to find more information.

1. Go to www.factsurfer.com.

2. Enter "Cinco de Mayo" into the search box and click .

3. Select your book cover to see a list of related content.

Index

battle, 10, 14
colored paper, 16
dance, 4, 20
learn, 14
life, 12
May, 6
Mexican, 8, 11, 12, 18

mole, 18, 19
music, 4, 20
paper flowers, 16, 17
parades, 20, 21
Puebla, 10, 11
tacos, 18

The images in this book are reproduced through the courtesy of: Pixel-Shot, front cover; Arlette Lopez, p. 3; Suzette Leg Anthony, pp. 4-5; miker, pp. 6-7; ZUMA Press Inc/ Alamy, pp. 8-9; Felix Lipov, pp. 10-11; Richard Levine/ Alamy, pp. 12-13; Alfredo Estrella/ Stringer/ Getty, pp. 14-15; Steve Skjold/ Alamy, pp. 16-17; bonchan, p. 18; Marcos Castillo, pp. 18-19; Dougberry, pp. 20, 23 (folk music); Chon Kit Leong/ Alamy, pp. 20-21; andresr, p. 22; dpa picture alliance/ Alamy, p. 22 (act out battle); photostar72, p. 22 (eat Mexican food); Jim West/ Alamy, p. 22 (go to parades); World History Archive/ Alamy, p. 23 (battle); etorres, p. 23 (mole); Ethel Wolvovitz/ Alamy, p. 23 (parades).